The little book of
BEAVER SCOUTS

First published 2011 by Macmillan Children's Books
a division of Macmillan Publishers Limited
20 New Wharf Road, London N1 9RR
Basingstoke and Oxford
Associated companies throughout the world
www.panmacmillan.com

ISBN 978-1-4472-0168-7

Printed and bound in the UK by CPI Mackays, Chatham ME5 8TD

Picture Credits

Pages 1, 5, 22, 23, 25, 46–49, 64, The Scout Association; page 18 Richard
Hammond courtesy of Ed Perchick and Wikimedia Commons; page 18
Barack Obama courtesy of Pete Souza, The Obama-Biden Transition
Project and Wikimedia Commons; page 19 Jamie Oliver courtesy of
Really Short and Wikimedia Commons; page 25 Baden-Powell courtesy
of flagsbay.com and Wikimedia Commons; page 37 courtesy of 1st
Longham Beaver Scout Colony.

The little book of BEAVER SCOUTS

Activities and fun facts just for you!

Amanda Li

MACMILLAN CHILDREN'S BOOKS

CONTENTS

INTRODUCTION

25 Years Is a Long Time!

I was only twelve when Beaver Scouting began
in 1986. My favourite things to do then were
climbing trees, camping out and going on long
walks around the island where I lived. Today I
still love going outdoors and I still love Scouting.

This book is to help celebrate Beaver
Scouting's very special birthday. It's full of fun,
games, jokes and facts – all about one thing:
Beavers! Did you know Beavers in Denmark
are called Micro Scouts? Did you know a baby
beaver animal is called a kit? Whether you've
just joined or have been a Beaver for a while,
this book will help you have more fun than ever.

Enjoy your adventures.

Your friend,

Bear

Bear Grylls
Chief Scout

WE ARE BEAVER SCOUTS

All About Us

- We're boys and girls aged between six and eight years old.
- Our uniform is a bright turquoise sweatshirt with a coloured scarf.
- Beaver Scouts usually meet up once a week in a Scout group known as a Colony.

All Beavers make a special Promise soon after they join:

The Beaver Scout Promise

I promise to do my best,
To be kind and helpful
And to love God.

This Is What We Do

- Beaver Scouts go outdoors, play games, make things, sing songs and make new friends. We go on visits to interesting places like zoos and theatres and we sometimes spend nights away from home.

'At Beavers, we play really fun games and it makes me feel happy.' **Miles, 6**

- We love to learn new things and there are lots of different Beaver Scout badges we can earn.
- There are Beaver Scout Colonies all over the UK. They all wear a uniform and share the same motto: **'Be prepared!'**

THE ADVENTURE BEGINS!

How Did Beavers Start?

More than a hundred years ago the Founder of Scouting, Lord Baden-Powell, organized the first ever Scout camp. On 1 August 1907, twenty boys began an eight-day camp on Brownsea Island, Dorset. The boys were divided into four patrols – Wolves, Bulls, Curlews and Ravens.

The skills the boys learned were:
• putting up tents
• building and lighting fires
• cooking food
• finding their way around by night and by day.

Scouts today still learn these skills.

After the camp Baden-Powell wrote a book called *Scouting for Boys* and he went around the country explaining his ideas. Within two years there were more than 100,000 Scouts in Britain.

At this time Scouts were all over the age of 11 – but it wasn't long before the younger brothers wanted to

Baden-Powell teaches new skills on Brownsea Island

join in too. So, in 1916, Baden-Powell began a new section of Scouting for boys aged 8 to 10. It was called the Wolf Cubs.

But what about the even younger ones? On 1 April 1986, boys aged 6 to 8 were finally able to join – as Beaver Scouts! In 1990, girls were allowed to join too. Girls had been able to join an older section of Scouting since 1976.

Today there are more than 31 million Scouts around the world, in 216 countries and territories. Each country has its own uniform and badges but we are all part of one big happy Scouting family.

THAT WAS THE YEAR . . .

Scouting has a long and interesting history. Here are just a few important dates:

1857 Robert Stephenson Smyth Powell is born (he later became known as Lord Baden-Powell).

1907 He organizes the first Scout camp on Brownsea Island.

1908 *Scouting for Boys* is published.

1909 The first Scout HQ is opened in London.

1916 The Wolf Cubs are launched and *The Wolf Cub's Handbook* is published.

1919 Gilwell Park in Essex is opened as a Scout camping and training centre.

1920 The first International Jamboree of Boy Scouts is held in London.

1923 The woggle is introduced to hold the scarf.

1966 The Wolf Cubs are given a new name – Cub Scouts.

1976 Girls join Venture Scouts.

1986 Beaver Scouts become official members of the Scout movement. Hooray!

1990 Girls are now allowed to join Beavers, Cubs and Scouts.

1995 Exciting new *Beaver Scout Challenge* badges are launched.

1996 *'Let's Party'* 10th birthday celebrations are held for Beaver Scouts everywhere.

2009 Bear Grylls becomes the new Chief Scout.

2011 The Scout Association celebrates 25 years of Beaver Scouting. Happy Birthday, Beavers!

THE LODGE OF LAUGHS!

Welcome to my Lodge of Laughs! Here are my favourite jokes about one of the world's greatest animals – the beaver, of course!

Which side of a beaver has the most fur?
The outside!

What do you call a beaver at the South Pole?
Lost!

What's furry, builds dams and is bright blue?
A beaver holding its breath!

How do beavers get online?
They log on!

What did the beaver say to the tree?

'It's been nice gnawing you!'

THE REAL BEAVERS

Like you, beavers have lots of talents. They can swim fast, build incredible dams, and they can even chop down trees with their sharp teeth!

Brilliant Beavers

Beavers live mostly in forests in North America and in some parts of Europe and Asia.

They are furry brown animals with large flat tails shaped like paddles. These tails are incredibly useful. Beavers use them as rudders to help them steer when they swim. They also use their tails to help make their homes – called lodges.

Beavers are extremely good at building things. They cut down trees and branches with their teeth and use the logs to build dams across rivers, making ponds. Then they cover the dam with mud, sticks and stones so that water can't escape. They use their flat tails to spread mud over the dam.

A real beaver

Did You Know?

- Baby beavers are called kits. By the time they are one month old they can swim well.

- Beavers live together in groups called colonies. Sound familiar?

- Beavers sometimes slap their tails hard against the water. This can be a way of saying 'welcome' to their friends. It can also be an alarm call, warning other beavers to be very careful.

- Beavers used to be hunted and they almost became extinct in the UK. But now they are being spotted again, mainly in parts of Scotland and South-West England.

ARE YOU LiKE A REAL BEAVER?

Read On and Find Out . . .

• An average-sized beaver weighs about 20 kilograms. How much do you weigh?

- -

• How many fingers and thumbs do you have on each hand? The beaver has the same number! He uses his front paws in the same way that you use your hands – to hold and grip things. The beaver is really good at building things with his hands. Are you?

- -

• Beavers are very good swimmers. Their back feet have webs between the toes to help them move through the water. Can you swim?

- -

- The beaver builds its own home using logs and mud. It floats on the water and has underwater entrances. It is called a lodge. What is your home called?

_____

- Beavers like eating leaves, bark, roots, wood and plants. What do you like to eat?

_____

- Beavers are friendly animals. When two beavers meet they make chattering noises and rub their cheeks together. Are you friendly?

_____

Beavers have fun and make friends – just like you!

BUSY BEAVERS

How to Draw a Beaver

1. Draw a circle for the beaver's head and an oval for his body.

2. Add a flat oval tail.

3. Now give him a face. Draw a nose, a mouth, eyes and ears. Don't forget his sharp teeth!

4. Add arms and legs. Then draw criss-cross lines on the beaver's tail.

5. Now colour in your beaver.

BEAVER FUN

Crossword Challenge

How much can you remember about beavers?
Write the answers across the puzzle. The word
'LODGE' will help you. Answers are on page 73.

CLUES

1. A beaver has a large flat _____ .

2. Beavers use sticks and _____ to help
   build a dam.

3. It's soft, mucky and is used to fill the gaps
   in a dam.

4. A piece of chopped wood is sometimes called
   a _____ .

5. A beaver's _____ are very sharp.

1			L		
2			O		
3			D		
4			G		
5			E		

A real lodge

FAMOUS SCOUTS

Many famous people were Scouts when they were young. Which of these famous Scouts have you heard of?

Steve Backshall – TV wildlife presenter

Billy Connolly – comedian and actor

David Attenborough – TV wildlife expert

Richard Hammond – TV presenter

Natasha Kaplinski – newsreader

Bear Grylls – explorer, author and UK Chief Scout

Barack Obama – current President of the United States

Richard Hammond

Barack Obama

Harrison Ford – the actor who plays Indiana Jones, and Han Solo (in the film *Star Wars*)

Mark Ramprakash – cricketer

Michael Owen – footballer

David Beckham – footballer

Andy Murray – tennis champion

Ray Mears – survival expert

Richard McCourt and Dominic Wood – of TV's Dick and Dom

Jamie Oliver

Jamie Oliver – TV chef

BEAVER BADGES

It's a very proud moment when you earn a new badge. Here are some tips for helping you to get some Beaver Scout badges.

The Hobbies Activity Badge

To earn this badge you need to take part in a hobby of your choice and tell your friends at Beavers all about it.

What Are Hobbies?

Hobbies are things that you enjoy doing in your spare time. If you haven't already got a hobby, just take a look at these ideas:

- Collecting – this could be a collection of trading cards, toys, shells, stamps, coins, etc. Some people collect unusual things like china frogs or novelty rubbers!

- Doing magic tricks
- Writing stories
- Lego building
- Cookery
- Reading
- Sewing
- Looking after a pet
- Swimming
- Tennis
- Skateboarding
- Football
- Cricket
- Tag rugby
- Gymnastics
- Dancing
- Painting, drawing and making things
- Making models – planes, cars, things made from wood or clay
- Playing a musical instrument
- Singing in a group or choir

What kind of hobbies do *you* have?

\- \-

Did you know that you can earn more than one Hobbies Activity Badge? So why not have more than one hobby!

ARE YOU A BRILLIANT BEAVER?

Try this mini-quiz to see how much you know about Beavers – both the Scouting and animal kind!

1. What are baby beavers called?
a. Kits
b. Calves
c. Kids

2. Our Chief Scout is called _____ Grylls.
a. Beaver
b. Bear
c. Buffalo

3. How can a Beaver Scout earn the Chief Scout's Bronze Award?
a. Tidying up after Colony meetings
b. Being kind and helpful all the time
c. Getting all the Beaver Scout Challenge Awards

4. What is unusual about the Beaver Scout handshake?
a. Beaver Scouts shake with their left hands
b. Beaver Scouts shake with their right hands
c. Beaver Scouts shake with both hands

5. The Scout motto is:
a. Be Kind
b. Be Helpful
c. Be Prepared

Now check your answers (on page 73) to find out your score. If you get three or more correct answers, you are a **Brilliant Beaver**!

FUN FACTS!

Beaver Scouts Around the World

• In Australia young Scouts are called Joey Scouts. A joey is a young kangaroo.

• In New Zealand they are called Kea Scouts – this is the name of a New Zealand bird.

• In Denmark they are called Micro Scouts.

• In Italy boys and girls can become Castarinos – the Italian word for 'beaver'.

• In the Netherlands there's not much difference – Beavers are called 'bevers'!

LORD BADEN-POWELL – THE ORIGINAL SCOUT

- Lord Baden-Powell was the Founder of the Scout movement. He was the first Chief Scout.

- Baden-Powell was very good at acting and painting. He was also very musical. When he was at school he played the piano, the violin and the bugle-horn *and* he sang in the choir.

- Baden-Powell had the nickname 'Bathing Towel' when he was at school!

'Friends of the World' by Baden-Powell

BEAVER BADGES

To get your **Beaver Scout Healthy Eating Activity Badge** you must make a fruit salad, two different sandwiches and some healthy snacks. Here are some ideas to help you:

Super Snacks

- Take a handful of berries and mix them into a bowl of yogurt.
- Spread some peanut butter on to a stick of celery and top with raisins – it will look like ants on a log!
- With the help of an adult, cut sticks of carrot, pepper or cucumber and dip them into hummus or cream cheese – mmm!

Fantastic Fruit Salad

Choose your favourite fruits. Try to use fruits of different colours so that your salad looks as good as it tastes. You could start with apples, grapes and bananas and add blueberries, strawberries or pineapple – or more unusual fruits such as mango and papaya.

With the help of an adult, cut the fruit into bite-sized pieces and place into a bowl with a little fruit juice. Mix up the pieces – being careful not to squash them – and enjoy your tasty treat.

Sensational Sandwiches

Take two slices of brown or wholemeal bread and spread them thinly with butter. Now for the tasty filling. Try any of the following:

- chicken
- egg
- tuna
- turkey
- ham
- grated cheese/ cream cheese
- hummus
- avocado

Add some crunchy extras – how about sliced cucumber, lettuce, tomato, cress, pepper or grated carrot? With the help of an adult, cut your sandwich into four quarters and serve – not only healthy but absolutely delicious!

BEAVER FUN

Tasty Wordsearch

Can you find these seven fruit and vegetables in the wordsearch? The words could be up, down, forwards, backwards or diagonal. Answers on page 73.

CARROT

TOMATO

PEPPER

APPLE

GRAPE

ORANGE

MANGO

```
A C A R R O T O U
E E G N A R O G M
M A A P O G M P L
A P G G U R A E V
G P P R B O T P I
B L P M A D O P Q
B E L I G P O E P
U O E M A R E R L
B M A N G O K K N
```

THE LODGE OF LAUGHS!

Hello again. Why don't you get your Colony chuckling with these funny animal jokes!

When is it bad luck to see a black cat?
When you're a mouse!

What day do fish hate?
Fry-day.

Where do cows go on Saturday nights?
To the MOO-vies!

What is the strongest animal?
A snail. He carries his house on his back!

What do you get when you cross a hedgehog with a balloon?
POP!

What time is it when an elephant sits on your fence?

Time to get a new fence!

TALK LIKE A BEAVER

Beaver Scouts and their leaders have a whole language of their own. Here are just a few words that might come in useful:

Activity Badge Beaver Scouts can earn these. Every badge is different but all the badges are about trying new things.

B-P Short for Lord Baden-Powell.

Challenge Award As the name suggests, these badges are a bit more challenging but just as much fun as Activity Badges. There are six different Challenge Awards to gain.

Chief Scout This person leads the Scout movement in the UK. Bear Grylls is the current Chief Scout.

Chief Scout's Bronze Award The top award for a Beaver who has gained all six Challenge Awards.

Colony A group of Beaver Scouts and their leaders.

Investiture A special ceremony for a new Beaver Scout who is making his/her Promise and joining the Colony.

Jamboree A big meeting of Scouts. In 2011 the World Scout Jamboree takes place in Sweden. In 2015 it will be in Japan.

Joining-in Award A badge awarded to a Beaver Scout for taking part in meetings. You usually get your first Joining-in Award when you have attended your Colony meetings for a year.

Lodge A smaller group of Beaver Scouts within a Colony.

Membership Award A badge awarded to a Beaver Scout when he/she has made the Promise and understands what being a Beaver Scout is all about.

Scout Salute A special salute used at ceremonies and meetings.

Swimming Up A ceremony for a Beaver Scout when he or she goes up to Cub Scouts.

Woggle A ring which holds the neck scarf together.

BUSY BEAVERS

Would you like to make your own Beaver Scout bookend? He or she will be able to sit on your bookshelf and stop your books from falling down.

Make a Beaver Bookend

You will need:

- a clean empty tub or small container with a lid – an empty gravy drum is ideal
- coloured felt or paper
- sand
- wool
- glue/sticky tape
- scissors
- felt-tip pens
- thin card (optional)

1. Fill your container with sand to make it nice and heavy and put on the lid. Secure it with tape.
2. Cover the top third of the container with felt or paper and glue it down. Use felt tips to

draw the eyes, nose and
mouth.

3. Cut lengths of wool for the hair
   and glue across the top of the
   head. Use your imagination to
   create a hairstyle.

4. Now for the uniform. Cover the
   rest of the container with blue
   felt or paper – this is the jumper.
   You can add a coloured-paper
   scarf and maybe glue on some
   pretend badges! Why not add
   a woggle by tying a piece of
   wool around the scarf?

5. To make your bookend even more realistic,
   glue on arms and legs made of felt or thin
   card. If you have two containers why not
   make two Beaver Scouts – one for each
   end of your
   bookshelf!

Brave Beavers

The skills that Beavers learn can come in very useful in everyday life. No one knows this better than eight-year-old Joshua, a brave Beaver Scout who helped his family escape from a very dangerous situation.

Joshua had joined the 1st Longham Beaver Scout Colony just a few weeks before the incident. One of the first things his Colony did was to learn all about fire safety. So when a serious fire broke out at his home during the night, Joshua knew what to do. He remembered that the Beaver Scout Leader had said that it was important to remain calm when evacuating a building. So, while his mum was helping his disabled younger sister to get out of the house, Joshua looked for his other younger sister, found her wandering about, and calmly led her out of the house to safety.

Now Joshua is one of the youngest members of The Scout Association to receive the Chief Scout's Commendation for Meritorious Conduct! This is a very special bravery award.

Proud Joshua receives his special award

Another quick-thinking Beaver to receive the same award was Jack, a Beaver Scout from the 4th Falmouth Scout Group. In 2007, Jack's dad badly hurt himself while working in the garden one day. Jack realized how serious the situation was and phoned 999 for an ambulance. He knew that he needed to stay calm and talk clearly. Jack's quick actions meant that his dad got the medical help he needed in time.

These two brave Beaver Scouts really deserved their awards!

What's the bravest thing you've ever done?

- -

BEAVER BADGES

To get your **Safety Activity Badge**, you must
know about road safety, water safety,
stranger danger and safety in the
home. Here are a few tips to start
you off.

Road Safety

Do you know how to cross a road safely? The
Green Cross Code will help you. Always

> STOP
>
> LISTEN
>
> LOOK
>
> THINK

before you cross a road. Keep on looking and
listening while you cross the road.

Why don't you make a colourful poster so
that all your friends can see the Green Cross
Code? Write the Code out in big bright letters
and draw pictures around it. You could take the
poster along to your next Colony meeting or ask
your teacher if you can put it up at school.

Safety In the Home

Take a look at this picture. There are lots of things in the room that could cause an accident. Can you find and circle five or more of them?

Answers are on page 73–4.

SLEEPY BEAVERS

Have you ever been away from home for a whole night before? Once you become a Beaver Scout you might get the chance to go camping for the first time. It might be an indoor camp, inside a Scout meeting place, or outside in a tent. You will go with your leaders and other adult helpers who will make sure you have a really good time!

What Happens on a Night Away?

Before you go you will be given a list of things to bring along and this will usually include a sleeping bag, pyjamas, a wash bag and a change of clothes for the next day.

Every camp is different but you will be told what time to arrive by your leader. There will be a chance to play games or do activities such as crafts with all the other Beaver Scouts. When all the games and activities have been played everyone might have something tasty to eat and drink (provided by your leader). Afterwards you might gather round and sing songs and there may even be a campfire outside. Later on, you will settle down for the night in your camp. Your leaders and grown-up helpers will sleep nearby but in a different room or area. There will probably be a lot of laughter going on as you all get ready for bed and into your sleeping bags. At some point your leader will say 'Lights out', but one thing's for sure – you will be going to sleep a lot later than you do at home!

In the morning, you'll be given a wake-up call (if you're not all awake already) and you'll have breakfast together. There might even be time for a few more games before you go home. You'll probably feel quite tired on the day after a night away so you might need an early night!

What's So Great About Nights Away?

- You get to know your Beaver Scout friends even better than before – it's an ideal time to find out something new about the others in your Colony.

- You can get a badge – the **Nights Away Staged Activity Badge** – for going away for one night and sleeping in a centre or a tent.

- It's so much fun! Being away from home for the night is very exciting, though you might feel a bit nervous at first. But you will quickly get used to it and will soon be looking forward to your next night away.

FUN FACTS ABOUT BEAVERS

More about our favourite animals:

- A beaver's lodge is a mound of sticks, stones and mud. It looks a bit like a giant hedgehog with prickles!

- Beavers have a set of transparent eyelids that they use as 'goggles'. This means they can see underwater with their eyes closed!

- They can stay underwater for up to fifteen minutes without needing to surface for air.

- In 2010, with the help of satellite technology, an ecologist spotted the largest beaver dam ever found. The dam is a massive 850 metres (2,788 ft) wide – the size of eight football pitches!

THE LODGE OF LAUGHS!

Leader: What did one flag say to the other flag?
Beaver Scout: I don't know.
Leader: Nothing. It just waved!

Why did the Beaver Scout take a tape measure to camp?
To see how long he slept!

What should a Beaver Scout do if he finds an elephant in his sleeping bag?
Sleep somewhere else!

Which is the best creature for a Beaver Scout to take camping?

Leader: Knock, knock.

Beaver Scout: Who's there?

Leader: Noah.

Beaver Scout: Noah who?

Leader: Noah how to put up a tent?

Why did the Beaver Scout sleep under a tractor?

She wanted to wake up oily in the morning!

Which is the best creature for a Beaver Scout to take camping?

The octopus – he has lots of tent-acles!

BEAVER FUNDAYS

If you've ever fancied climbing through a giant web or building a water rocket, a Funday could be just your thing! Fundays are action-packed activity days which are held at Gilwell Park, on the edge of Epping Forest in London, and many other places. There are lots and lots of things for Beaver Scouts to do.

'We're going to our first Funday soon and I'm really looking forward to it!' **Poppy, 6**

Here are just a few of the activities on offer at a Funday:

Aerial Runway

Whizz along an overhead line.

Pedal Go-karting

Control your own go-kart and ride around a real track.

Grass Sledging

Keep your arms and legs in the sled as you zoom down the grass course on a special sledge.

Water Slides

Whizz down a very wet slide and enjoy the ride as the water helps you speed along!

Water Rockets

Your rocket is a used plastic drinks bottle. Make your rocket fly upwards as air forces the water out and the rocket up!

Robot Wars

Action-packed radio-controlled fun! Control your robot in a one-on-one battle with another robot. Who will win?

Spider Mountain

Climb and scramble your way up through this giant criss-crossed 'web'. Not as easy as it looks!

Jump Mats

Jump to your heart's content on these soft mats.

There's also face painting, bouncy castles, a fairground, food and lots more. So what are you waiting for? Ask your leader when the next Fundays are happening.

49

PERFECT PARTIES

When you're a Beaver Scout, you don't need an excuse to have a party! Here are some great game ideas for your next get-together.

Balloon Juggling

You will need: Lots of balloons.

Objective: To keep as many balloons in the air as possible.

Rules: You may only TAP the balloons – no grabbing or holding.

How to play: This game is super-simple! Everyone is given a balloon and on 'Go!' they throw their balloons up in the air and keep

them up as long as possible by tapping and gently knocking them. If a player's balloon touches the ground they are out! The last player left is the winner.

Funny Faces

You will need: A sheet of newspaper and scissors.

Objective: To make the funniest face possible!

How to play: Cut a hole in the centre of the sheet. Each person takes it in turn to hold up the paper, puts their head through the hole and pulls a funny face. Decide on a set time, and the person who pulls the most funny faces in that time is the winner. Give another prize for the funniest face.

BUSY BEAVERS

Make a Trophy

Whatever games and sports you're playing, it's fun to make a pretend trophy for the winner.

You will need:

- a clean empty tin can
- some tin foil
- paper
- glue
- scissors

1. First make the figure for the top of the trophy. Cut or tear a piece of the tin foil about 15 cm x 20 cm. Make five tears in the foil.

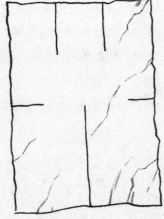

2. Now fold the foil up as shown, and scrunch up into a head, arms and legs.

3. Bend the bottoms of the legs to make feet and twist them into a pose. Your figure can be doing any activity you want – playing football, skating, playing cricket, dancing, etc. You could also make a ball from a small piece of scrunched-up foil.

4. Cover your tin can in paper and glue it down. Now turn it upside down and glue your sporty figure on to the top, ready for a presentation!

BEAVER FUN

Word Puzzle

Take a look at these questions. All the answers are made from letters in the word

BEAVER

1. A buzzing insect that makes honey.

   _ _ _

2. It's on the side of your head and you use it for listening. You have two of these.

   _ _ _

3. Polar, Grizzly and Teddy are all one of these!

   _ _ _ _

4. A _ _ _ of chocolate is a delicious treat.

Answers are on page 74.

Draw the Uniform

Can you finish this picture of a Beaver Scout by drawing the uniform? You'll need to draw the shirt, scarf and trousers. Don't forget his/her hair – and maybe a cap and some badges!

THE LODGE OF LAUGHS!

What do you give an elephant that's going to be sick?

Plenty of space!

What do you call a dancing cow?

A milkshake!

What are the wettest animals in the world?

Reindeer!

What kind of snake is good at maths?

How do you get in touch with a fish?

Drop him a line!

What do cats eat for breakfast?

Mice crispies!

What kind of snake is good at maths?

An adder!

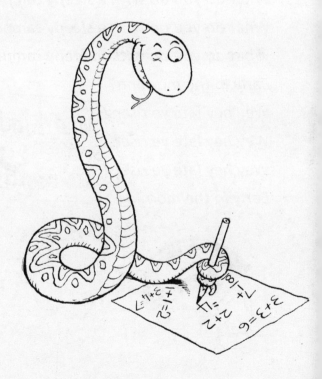

SiNG, BEAVERS, SiNG!

Here are some funny songs to sing at Colony meetings or nights away:

Sleepy Camper

(Sing to the tune of 'Drunken Sailor')

What do you do with a sleepy camper?
What do you do with a sleepy camper?
What do you do with a sleepy camper
Early in the morning?
Wey hey late ye risers!
Wey hey late ye risers!
Wey hey late ye risers!
Early in the morning.

Super Lizard

(Sing this one to the tune of 'Frère Jacques')

Super lizard
Super lizard
See him swim
See him swim
In and out the water
In and out the water
With his fins
With his fins.

Row Row Row Your Boat

Row row row your boat
Gently down the stream
Ha ha, fooled you
I'm a submarine!

Busy Beavers

Making Music

Why not accompany yourselves while you're singing? Here's how to make some easy musical instruments for meetings and on camping trips.

Bang the Drums

To make deep notes, stretch a piece of cling film over a small bucket or wastepaper bin. Use an elastic band over the top of the cling film to keep the 'skin' stretched tight. Bang the drum with your fingertips.

For smaller drums, use clean jam-jars or the cardboard tubes from kitchen rolls. You'll find they make a higher sound.

Shake Your Maracas

Fill two clean empty washing-up liquid bottles with dried peas, rice or lentils. Hold one in each hand – and shake! Try sugar or sand for a slightly different sound.

Glass Bells

You will need some clean glasses – up to eight. Put the glasses in a row on a table. Using a jug of water, pour different amounts of water into each glass. Start with about 3 cm of water in the first glass, add a little more to the next glass and so on. Now tap each glass with a metal spoon. You should be able to hear a range of different notes. If you have eight bottles you might be able to produce 'doh-ray-me-fah-soh-lah-te-doh'!

Crash Your Cymbals

This one's easy – just get two saucepan lids and bang them together!

BEAVER FUN

Spot the Difference

Look at the two pictures. Can you find six differences between them? You can colour in the pictures afterwards. Answers are on page 74.

ALL-ACTiON BEAVERS

There are so many activities that you will get the chance to do as a Beaver Scout! Tick the boxes of the ones you've done!

☐ Onwards and Upwards

Anyone can climb – start off on a low climbing wall to get your confidence. Climbing walls have all kinds of lumps and bumps for you to hold on to and put your feet on, as you make your way upwards. Later on, you will wear a harness if you want to try a more challenging wall. It's a fantastic feeling when you get to the top!

☐ Whizzing on Wheels

Can you ride a bike yet? Cycling is a great way to get around. So is riding on a scooter or whizzing along on rollerblades. Some Colonies have special 'wheely' nights, when Beaver Scouts bring along their own bikes, scooters

64

and helmets, and ride a small course together. It's 'wheely' good fun!

☐ Watery Fun

If you've never been on a boat before, bell boating is a really good activity for beginners. A bell boat is like two boats joined together, with a small deck in the centre. Up to twelve people can get on board. Following your leader's instructions, you have to work together as a team to paddle your boat along. It's a great way to learn skills for canoeing and kayaking.

There are many other ways to enjoy the water too. For example, a group of Beaver Scouts might try building a small raft that will take a teddy bear along a stream. Ready, teddy, go!

☐ Go for a Walk

All you need is a pair of comfortable shoes and you're off! There are all kinds of hikes you might do in a group. Walking through woods and forests, going on nature trails and hiking up hills are just a few ways of enjoying the great outdoors.

BEAVER FUN

All-action Crossword

How much do you know about outdoor activities? If you're not sure about the answers, look back at pages 64 and 65. Answers are on page 74.

Across

2. Most people learn to climb on a climbing ____ .

3. A _____ boat is a special boat with a central deck.

4. To do this, all you need are some comfy shoes!

Down

1. If you're riding a bike or a scooter you should wear one of these on your head.

2. Bikes have two of these – without them you won't get far!

25 YEARS TO REMEMBER

Beaver Scouts officially began in 1986. The year 2011 is special for Beaver Scouts because it marks their 25th anniversary. What has happened in the world since then? Here are just a few events:

In **1986** Pixar Studios opens – they would go on to make such films as *Toy Story*, *Finding Nemo*, *Cars* and *Monsters Inc*. In sport, Argentina beats England 2–1 in a tense World Cup football match.

In **1989** after dividing East and West Germany for 28 years, the Berlin Wall falls and the country is reunited.

In **1990** Nelson Mandela is released from prison in South Africa after being held for more than 27 years. British computer scientist Sir Timothy Berners-Lee creates the World Wide Web.

In **1994** the Channel Tunnel is opened between England and France. Nelson Mandela becomes South Africa's first black President.

In **1997** *Harry Potter and the Philosopher's Stone* by J. K. Rowling is published.

In **1999** the Euro currency is first introduced (although the UK keeps pounds and pence). On 31 December millennium celebrations take place throughout the world. The twenty-first century has arrived!

In **2002** Queen Elizabeth's Golden Jubilee is celebrated.

In **2004** the 60th anniversary of D-Day is remembered. On Boxing Day a massive tsunami hits fourteen Asian countries, creating waves up to 30 metres high.

In **2009** Senator Barack Obama becomes President of the United States – the first African-American President.

In **2010** a volcanic ash cloud from Iceland disrupts air travel around the world. In Chile 33 miners survive underground for 69 days.

In **2011** Prince William and Kate Middleton are married. Beaver Scouts celebrate their 25th anniversary!

Why We Love Being Beavers!

'I love Beavers because of the fun and games we have. We learn about things and get badges.'
Mollie, 6

'This year we went to see a coastguard helicopter. All the Beavers got to go inside and we all had great fun. I wanted to fly it, but they wouldn't let me – not yet!' **Philip, 7**

'I love all the great games we play.' **Claire, 7**

'I like how we have a Promise and a Salute at our meetings. And I like doing art and making things.' **Sanjay, 6**

JOIN THE BEAVER SCOUT ADVENTURE

If you are not already a Beaver Scout and would like to have fun and make friends, then ask your parents to fill in their details at **www.scouts.org.uk/join**. A local leader will call back with the details.

We always need more volunteers to help more young people join in the fun – Beaver Scouting is great fun for adults too. Find out more at **www.scouts.org.uk/join**.

A Goodbye Song

Here's a little song that some Beaver Scouts sing at the end of their Colony meetings. Why don't you learn it too?

1 – 2 – 3,
Who are we?
We are Beavers, can't you see?
B – E – A – V – E – R – S, (say the letters out loud)
Beavers, beavers are the best!

BEAVER FUN

Colouring In

Beaver Scouts play lots of different games. Can you colour in this picture of two Beaver Scouts having fun? Make sure their scarves are the same colour as your Colony's.

ANSWERS TO PUZZLES

Page 16 Beaver Fun – Crossword Challenge
1. TAIL; 2. STONES; 3. MUD; 4. LOG; 5. TEETH.

Page 22 Are you a Brilliant Beaver?
1a; 2b; 3c; 4a; 5c.

Page 28 Beaver Fun – Tasty Wordsearch

Page 39 Safety in the Home
There are twelve obstacles that could cause an accident in this picture. How many did you find?

1. The smoke alarm has no batteries and is not working.
2. A bottle of bleach has been left out – it should be locked away from small children.
3. A cloth is hanging over the hob, which might catch fire.
4. The saucepan handle is too close to the edge of the hob and might be knocked off, burning someone.
5. The drawer has been left open and could trip someone up.
6. The toaster flex is dangling in the sink – water and electricity together are *very* dangerous.
7. A sharp knife is sticking out from the worktop.
8. The floor is wet and slippery.
9. A candle is burning close to the curtain, which could catch fire.

10. A dog's lead is lying across the floor and could trip someone up.
11. There are too many plugs coming from one electrical socket, which could cause a fire. Also, the appliances have been left right in front of the door for someone to fall over.
12. The coffee maker is too close to the edge of the worktop and could be knocked off and burn someone.

Page 54 Beaver Fun – Word Puzzle
1. Bee; 2. Ear; 3. Bear; 4. Bar.

Page 62 Beaver Fun – Spot the Difference

Page 66 Beaver Fun – All-action Crossword
Across: 2. wall; 3. bell; 4. walk.
Down: 1. helmet; 2. wheels.